D1266435

The
IMPOSSIBLE
Major Rogers

The IMPOSSIBLE Major Rogers

by Patricia Lee Gauch

drawings by Robert Andrew Parker

G.P. Putnam's Sons · New York

ACKNOWLEDGMENTS

For their careful and generous assistance I wish to thank John Cuneo, author of the definitive biography, *Robert Rogers of the Rangers*, and Howard H. Peckham, director of the William L. Clements Library, University of Michigan, and editor of *Journals of Major Robert Rogers*. Further, I wish to acknowledge the influence of *Northwest Passage*, the fictional account of Robert Rogers by Kenneth Roberts, which set me off on my adventure.

Text copyright © 1977 by Patricia Lee Gauch
Illustrations copyright © 1977 by Robert Andrew Parker
All rights reserved. Published simultaneously in Canada by Longman Canada, Toronto. Printed in the United States of America.

Library of Congress Cataloging in Publication Data.

Gauch, Patricia Lee. The Impossible Major Rogers.
1. Rogers, Robert, 1731–1795—Juvenile literature. 2. United States—History—French and Indian War, 1755–1763—Juvenile literature. 3. Soldiers—United States—Biography—Juvenile literature. [1. Rogers, Robert, 1731–1795. 2. Soldiers. 3. United States—History—French and Indian War, 1755–1763] I. Parker, Robert Andrew. II. Title   E199.R74G38   973.2′6′0924   [B]
76-51233   ISBN-O-399-20593-4

for my son John
a follower, indeed, of the famous major

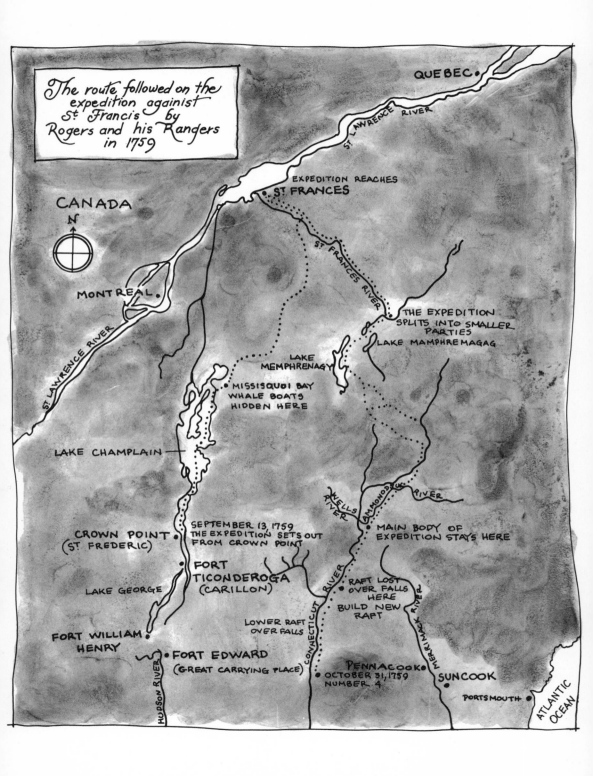

1

Robert Rogers was impossible. Even back in the 1700's, when a wilderness village was no more than six log houses and an animal pen, Robert Rogers was impossible.

He did the impossible. He said the impossible (to impossible people). He dreamed the impossible. And he was impossible to figure out, even back in the 1700's.

No one could honestly say, "Ah, that Robert Rogers is a good, good man," (though people often did). And no one could say, "Oh, that Rogers is a terrible scoundrel!" (though a good many said that, too). Because Robert Rogers wasn't exactly a good, good man or a terrible scoundrel.

He was . . . well . . . impossible.

And a body could only say one thing for certain about the man—and that was that he mattered. Back in the 1700's, when the frontier hung like a juicy plum between the French and English colonies, Robert Rogers mattered a good deal.

Of course, in the very beginning, in 1731, no one much took notice of Robert Rogers at all, except maybe his mother, Mary, his father, James, and his brothers,

Sam, James, and Daniel. That was the year Robert was born in a drafty, rough-hewn hut in Methuen, Massachusetts.

And to be honest, there wasn't much to note in the boy the next few years either. He and his family pushed north to the colony of New Hampshire. He plowed the fields and milked the cow and took pleasure in hunting his supper (pheasant, rabbit, coon) like any other frontier boy.

Oh, at 13 he already stretched to near six feet. That was worth noting since most men never reached five feet seven in those days. And the boy did appear to get uncommon pleasure at a house raising or corn husking where he challenged all comers in wrestling. When he "carried the ring"—that means outwrestling everyone—he did look a good bit like a young Tom Turkey strutting the yard.

Even so, Robert Rogers might have turned out to be just another rough-and-tumble frontier boy. But then 1745 came, and the Abenaki happened to Robert Rogers. Really happened to him. And from then on Robert Rogers was never just another rough-and-tumble frontier boy.

The Abenaki were Christian Indians led by the French. Ever since 1682, they and the English settlers had been attacking each other. They wanted the same land. The Abenaki struck and burned Deerfield. The English struck and burned Norridgewock. Sometimes their battling got so fierce it grew into a full-fledged war. Queen Anne's War, one was called. King William's, another. Or just plain—another French and Indian War.

Robert knew all about this feuding between the Abenaki and English over land. But it seemed pretty far away until 1745. That was the year the Abenaki started raiding the towns near him—Hopkinton, Suncook, Epsom. The Rogers family scurried into a town garrison—a kind of wooden fort—with all the other townsfolk. And for a while the trouble still seemed pretty far away, because Robert was kept inside the garrison with the other kids, the squalling babies and yapping dogs, while the men took turns patrolling the wilderness.

Then in August a howling war party ambushed eight town militiamen and scalped five of them not two miles from the garrison.

That close!

Robert refused to stay tucked away behind the safe walls any longer. The misty morning after the ambush, he sneaked out of the garrison and talked the captain into letting him join the town militia. He was only fourteen years old, but he had a quick tongue and a whole lot of anger.

It was only the beginning.

Robert stayed with the militia on and off for a year, seeing no Indians, and when the townsfolk trudged back to their homes for the winter of 1747–48, Robert went, too. It seemed so peaceful. In the spring, when the other townsfolk trickled back to the garrison and his father stubbornly refused to hurry back, Robert even stayed on at the farm with his family. It was that peaceful.

Or so it seemed.

In early May in the middle of the night, there came a thumping at the door. A townsman shouted, "Abenaki! Quick, to town. To town!"

The whole family moved fast enough then. Mary threw a few pots and pans into a cloth, James grabbed his gun, Robert picked up little Mollie (she was three) and off they stumbled into the darkness. And they were no five minutes from the garrison. They were ten miles away! Luckily, the moon shone and showed up the trail

marks chipped on the trees and they made it to the garrison, but not before they saw smoke curling up into the gray night sky from the direction of their cabin.

The next morning Robert and his father and four brothers went back to find everything in ashes—the tiny cabin, the shed barn, the apple trees—even Bess, their only milk cow.

Robert Rogers poked a stick angrily over and over in the ashes. There was nothing else to do. The Abenaki were gone. But he wouldn't forget. Not for a minute would Robert Rogers forget. He'd meet the Abenaki again all right, and he'd meet them face to face.

2

That was the way with Robert Rogers. When he took a notion into his head, he wasn't apt to forget it. But in 1748 the Abenaki stopped raiding. The king in England and the king in France agreed the war was over. All over. For the moment there was nothing to be done.

So, after all those months behind garrison walls, marching and marching through empty woods, rebuilding the farm, Robert Rogers was free to live a little. And he was ready.

He wanted money, for certain! Money to buy land, to gamble a little and to buy a little rum. That was the kind of man Rogers was, too. No mistaking it. And, of course, he was ready for some excitement.

So, not long after the battling was over, Rogers decided that the quickest way to get money—and excitement as well—would be to trade with his old enemies, the French and the Indians.

Since the English and all the colonists had been enemies of the French and the Abenaki Indians for so long, this was not legal at all. It wasn't even called trading; it was called smuggling. But that didn't bother Robert Rogers.

Off he set, alone, walking over hundreds and hundreds of miles of wilderness and mountains and bogs with only his musket, his knapsack and his quick tongue.

He didn't even know how to speak Abenaki or French since there's not much talk between enemies. But that didn't bother him either. Before he had made three trips he had "traded" enough furs and goods to feel a good deal of money jingling in his pocket, and he was laughing and cursing and arguing with the Abenaki and the French just as well as with his own people.

Of course that was one of those times some folks called him a terrible scoundrel. And it was true, if he had gotten caught, the governor could have sent him right to jail. But he didn't get caught and he did get to know how to survive in the wilderness. He got to know the streams, bogs, woods and mountain passes of the New England frontier. He got to know Frenchmen, and he got to know Indians, their language, how they thought and hunted and lived.

And he never, ever forgot.

That didn't matter right then. It was a peaceable time and Rogers even tried some properly peaceable pastimes. He tried surveying new land. He tried farming. But then he got itchy again. He had gotten to like the jingle of coins in his pockets, so one day when a crusty, scarred counterfeiter met him in the woods and asked him if he would like a good deal of money all for himself, Robert said he would indeed.

The trouble was the man had made the money himself, on his own machine, with his own bottles of ink, so that his money was no better than so many scraps of paper. But it looked real, so Robert Rogers tried to pass it along to his friends, saying he'd trade one cow for one note.

Before three months were over, Robert Rogers was dragged off to jail (it was really a neighbor's barn) and brought before the town justices. "I surely didn't know the money was counterfeit!" he told them, always the talker.

But John Stark, his best friend, was a talker, too, and not much of a liar! He had to admit to the judge that Robert Rogers had a notion in his head—to make quick money—and he was not at all happy it hadn't worked!

It seemed like this was the last notion Robert would be getting into his head for a while.

But it wasn't! It was while he was sitting in jail that he got his next one. And though it started small enough, no bigger than smuggling or counterfeiting, it grew until everyone knew about Robert Rogers and what he had in mind!

3

The small enough notion was that Robert Rogers decided that the army was the life for him. Another French and Indian War had burst out, the fourth one since 1690. Being stubborn and scrappy, he was determined right off that no French and Abenaki were going to burn his family and neighbors off their land again!

Besides, the judge hinted that if he joined the New Hampshire militia, the judge might forget all about the trial. That was good news!

So he took right to this new notion, small though it was. He even decided he'd be a captain (he never was much of a follower, for certain), and off he set with his musket, his knapsack, and his quick tongue to raise his own company. He beat the drums so loud and talked such a streak that when he joined up with the rest of the New Hampshire troops, he had raised not ten men like some recruiters, not sixteen men like others, but fifty men, including his friend, honest John Stark, and his own younger brother, Richard.

Captain Rogers they called him, and he liked it a good deal.

ROBERT A. PARKER
PUBLISHERS GRAPHICS

For the next five months he was happy being just Captain Rogers, one of 78 or so captains of the 3,500 or so provincial troops, which is what they called the soldiers from the colonies. Happy passing time on the way to the Great Carrying Place (later called Fort Edward). Happy doing nothing too special. Telling tales. Shooting game. Checking the wilderness now and then.

But then, just after the New Hampshirites reached the Great Carrying Place, September 8 came! The French and Abenaki sneaked up on the nearby British camp at Lake George and attacked it—it was the first attack of the new war—and the general, General William Johnson, got mad! As a general can.

He had been shot in the leg, but even from his bed inside the tent everyone knew General Johnson was mad. He raged about the mountains that separated him from the French and Indian enemies. He raged about the thick woods he couldn't see through. Where were the French and Abenaki? How many of them were there? How could he fight back when he didn't know where they were?

"Call the Mohawks!" he finally shouted. The Mohawk Indians were as loyal to the English as the Abenaki were to the French. They particularly liked Johnson. But they were going hunting just then.

"All right, then," he raged on, "Call someone like an Indian!"

That's when they called Captain Robert Rogers and he

liked it a good deal.

At first only he and a few men went out scouting for the general. Not many of the soldiers were too keen on getting caught in the wilds of enemy territory. But right off one thing was clear. Rogers had been long in hating the Abenaki, but he had been long in admiring them, too. Dressed in little more than a hide shirt and leggings (like Indians), he and four scouts skimmed the night lake in a canoe (like Indians). They sneaked through the shadowy woods. They threaded between the mountains until they crawled right into enemy territory—just like Indians.

Hiding behind trees, behind rocks and in bushes, Rogers drew pictures in his mind. A fort at Crown Point; sentry boxes, here; bastions, there; six chimneys, a draw-bridge and a moat, there. He counted barracks—three. He counted farmhouses nearby—10. He counted men— 500 French and 200 Abenaki, armed.

Three days after returning, he sneaked into enemy territory again. At the place called Ticonderoga, he dis-covered the French building a huge new fort, shaped like a star. Fort Carillon, someone called it. And more men, maybe 2,000 French "regular" soldiers! (Regular meant soldiers trained properly and especially to be soldiers.)

On the return trip he spotted a canoe with a Frenchman and five Indians just feet away from him and his men. Rogers and his scouts fired and, hopping into their canoe, pushed off after the French and Indians. The two canoes skimmed the water, Rogers drawing closer and closer,

only to discover two more enemy canoes racing toward them.

Rogers whipped his canoe around and outpaddled them, but he had discovered something. He could not only spy like Indians, he could fight like them.

All winter Rogers and his scouts sneaked back and forth carefully, cleverly picking up information and plans. General Johnson was delighted. Finally, he knew something. Too many French and Indians faced his untrained provincial troops. He'd wait for *British* regular troops to come, regulars with their polished guns, their training, their discipline, their cannon. His troops could finish building the fort while they waited.

But Rogers couldn't wait. Ever since that first scout into enemy territory his notion had started to grow. Now it started bursting out of him at every turn. He shared it with his friend John Stark on the parade ground. He shared it with his brother Richard in their tent. He even shared it with the judge's son, Joe Blanchard. Why, he figured, if three men could sneak in and out of the wilderness like Indians, why not a *company* of men? Why not!

But the more itchy Captain Rogers got, the more cautious General Johnson got. Finally, General Johnson, seeing the first flakes of winter, packed up the troops and his Mohawks and went home. Two hundred and thirty-eight men stayed on to people the winter fort now called Fort William Henry. But Robert Rogers didn't want to just people the fort. Abenaki Indians sometimes attacked and scouted in winter! Why couldn't he?

So, with only a colonel in command of the winter fort, and before any general could say no, Rogers talked thirty-two men into going on with him, not just to scout but to cut off enemy supplies as well. Thirty-two men whom Rogers was certain knew the wilderness as he did —how the moss grew on the north side of the tree, where the lily bulbs grew for eating, how to shoot a rabbit in the bush. Rangers he called them.

Nothing would stop them. Not snow, not sleet, not freezing temperatures, not icy wilderness. Of course nobody exactly promised to pay these men, but there was no time to worry now. Nothing would stop Rogers and his rangers. Not now.

In early December in a blizzardy snow, the captain and three men spied on the new star-shaped fort at Ticonderoga. Three days later he and seventeen men ice-skated across Lake Champlain to ambush a sleigh of food. They chopped a hole and dropped the cargo of beef into it. No French or Abenaki would eat that beef!

Ten days later he led fifty men (he borrowed a few) to the fort at Crown Point, where they dashed here and there over the countryside, setting fire to grain-filled barns, farmhouses, capturing prisoners for information!

On and on Rogers and his new rangers went, appearing and disappearing, whooping like Indians, darting in and out of enemy territory in the thick of winter. There was no one like his rangers, not to Captain Rogers. You need money, rangers? Here, take some. Your feet are freezing! I'll wrap them. You ride in the sleigh, ranger; I'll walk.

Newspapers in Boston and New York also thought there was no one like Rogers and his rangers: "Captain Rogers with his party of men . . . have burned a great many (enemy) barns; Captain Rogers stayed but one day in the fort and set out (again) . . . 125 Spanish dollars sent to the brave Captain Rogers." The British and the colonists needed some good news about then. Papers even had Rogers and his rangers doing things they hadn't done. In their stories Robert Rogers was ten feet tall.

Likely, it was all this success that set Rogers' notion growing again. Because sometime that winter it started. Why, he told his brother Richard, who always, always listened . . . why, if we can strike with twenty or twenty-five frontiersmen, why not raise special companies of rangers? Train them especially. Uniform them especially. *Ir*regulars! Why not? he dreamed. If they were the right men, they could cut communications, destroy supply lines, get information. Was there anything these rangers couldn't do? No, he agreed promptly with himself. Nothing.

Then, amazingly, before the winter was over, Rogers discovered someone else had almost the same idea. Someone important! General William Shirley, head of the whole British Army in North America.

He sent for Rogers to tell him. And Rogers went, posthaste, with his quick tongue, and before three days had passed, there they sat having tea and agreeing, the great man Shirley in his starched collar and lacy cuffs and the scruffy, scrappy frontiersman Rogers.

They talked over crumpets. They talked over tea. They talked when the cups were empty. And when they were done, the general said, "By Gad, I knew rangers were just what we needed! Why didn't I think of it before?" And he wrote a note which said Robert Rogers should raise an "Independent company of rangers, sixty privates, only courageous men experienced in hunting, tracking and long marches, three shillings a day."

Of course Captain Rogers agreed with every word of the note, but he got in one last word as well. He talked the general into sending New England whaleboats all the way over the mountains to Lake George. Canoes were too small for the ideas Robert Rogers had!

4

By now the French and Abenaki troops had strung themselves all the way from Canada to the fort at Ticonderoga. The British troops stood sturdily at Fort William Henry. Both sides kept getting more men, more guns, more cannon. Both sides kept getting stronger and stronger. They knew whoever won this war would win all of North America.

But neither side made a move!

Generals came and went like the seasons. General Loudoun replaced General Shirley, General Abercromby replaced General Loudoun, General Amherst replaced Abercromby. (Or was it General Abercromby who replaced General Amherst and General Shirley who replaced General Loudoun? It was hard to tell; they changed so often.)

Anyway, like General Johnson, mostly they all stewed. Shall we attack now? Or wait for the spring? Shall we attack now? Or wait for more regular troops?

The king in England was furious. He wanted action! Still the generals waited.

Robert Rogers didn't wait for anything. Before the

year 1756 was up, he had four companies of rangers, including thirty Stockbridge Indians. By 1758 he had five more companies and the rangers had their own snappy green uniforms with cocky feathered bonnets. (Some said they looked a good deal like the Scots, which was fitting enough since a good many of the rangers had descended from the Scots.) They had their own muskets and knives. They even had their own island in the Hudson River, right next to Fort Edward.

And while the rest of the army waited, grumbled, and waited some more, Rogers and his rangers slipped in and out of enemy territory in greater and greater numbers, raiding more and more, keeping their eyes on the enemy.

Even at their island camp Rogers kept the rangers on their toes. He drilled them every night, led them in shooting practice, taught them how to ambush and attack, how to retreat. And he insisted—sometimes at the top of his lungs—that the rangers stay alert and fit!

The provincials and regulars waiting for something to happen liked what Rogers was making happen. They even liked Rogers' scrappy—sometimes outright cocky— ways. Take that time Rogers spied the French sentry deep in enemy territory.

The Frenchman called out, "*Qui êtes-vous?*" (That means "Who are you?")

"*Des amis!*" Rogers answered in his pretty good French. ("Some friends!")

The sentry let Rogers and his men walk closer and

closer until he spotted the green uniforms. Then he shouted again, puzzled, *"Qui êtes-vous?"*

And Rogers laughed out, "Rogers!" and he cut off the sentry's breeches and marched him, posthaste and pantless, to camp. Needless to say, the fellow did not run away.

Again, not too long after, talk buzzed around camp when Rogers and thirty rangers crept behind French lines to destroy supplies at a French farm near Crown Point. When they had burned the farm and destroyed the grain, Rogers took a piece of paper, scratched a note, stuck it on a post and dashed away with his rangers.

The French general opened the note in the morning.

It read: Just to keep your records straight—'received' goods in quantity of three barrels of grain, five cows and a barn!

"Braggart!" the French general stormed the next day. "Braggart!"

But back at the British camp everyone enjoyed Rogers' "braggadocio." They liked his nerve, too, particularly on the foray to Crown Point in January 1757.

By then the French and Indians and Rogers and his rangers had gotten to know each other's ways too well. They had ambushed each other. They had scalped each other. They had captured each other.

That January the enemy troops trapped Rogers and eighty-three Rangers in a valley near Crown Point. Rogers himself was wounded in the head with a musket ball.

Raked with musket fire for hours, the bleeding Rogers

whistled his rangers to retreat, and they stumbled across the slippery snow to higher ground to wait for nightfall.

The French starting calling him, coaxing him. "Rogers!" they sang out. "Good Captain Rogers! Come over. We'll treat you kindly, Rogers."

"Rogers," the voice echoed.

But it didn't take Rogers long to give them an answer: a laugh that rolled over the darkening valley like an angry drum.

That night, completely encircled by French and Indians, Rogers and his rangers slipped through the net. Only thirteen men were lost.

Rogers was as slippery as an apple in a tub of lard, and the soldiers at Fort William Henry and Fort Edward delighted in it. But it was more than that for the generals. They were amazed at the way the rangers fought in the wilderness. The regular generals would cluck to their regular colonels (who clucked to their regular captains), "See that your regulars learn their secrets!" Or to Captain Rogers, "Why don't you write a book on wilderness fighting?" (Which he did, and he enjoyed it a good deal.)

They even started a whole new regiment in the regular army that was supposed to learn to fight like rangers! Light infantry they called it. They put a Colonel Thomas Gage in charge.

For a lot of months, to a lot of people—plain soldier, captain, colonel, general—Robert Rogers stood ten feet tall.

5

But times were changing.

As Rogers recruited more and more men, he couldn't be quite so picky. He and his brother took on all sorts to fill the ranger ranks—sailors, drifters, adventurers. Not an easy bunch to keep in tow. Sometimes, then, particularly when Rogers wasn't around, the rangers got a bit too lively, drank a bit too much rum, shouted a bit too loud, thought they were a bit too powerful. Like the time Rogers was recovering from the smallpox, the rangers grew angry at the regular British commander for jailing a young ranger and stormed the jail!

Some colonels and some generals started saying among themselves, "those rangers are nothing but ignorant, wild, brawling scoundrels. Good for nothing!" (You may be sure they didn't say that when Rogers was around!)

As for Rogers himself—well, when a man has the success Rogers had and is as cocky, scrappy, and stubborn as he, there's bound to be some people who don't like him. As time went on, some of the regular colonels took a dislike to Rogers matched only by their dislike for the French and Indians! But no one did much about it, except mumble, whisper, and write a few notes to each other.

Then March 1758 came.

If there was anyone who did not think Rogers stood ten feet tall, it was Colonel Haviland, head of Fort Edward. Every time he and Rogers passed in the fort yard, they bristled. The colonel must have been terribly weary of hearing Robert Rogers and all his big ideas about his rangers, because he ordered the cocky captain and his whole cocky group (400 of them) out to attack Crown Point. It was as if he were saying, "Well, let's see what you can do."

That was a first for Rogers. Never before had Rogers and his rangers been ordered to attack like an army.

And Rogers might have been happy (couldn't his rangers do anything?), but a provincial soldier was lost the night before Rogers was to leave. What if the Indians had captured him and the man had spilled the rangers' plans?

The colonel ordered the rangers to go anyway. And to make matters worse, he reduced the number of rangers from 400 to 181!

Well, 181 rangers, including the Stockbridge Indians, skated past Lake George. One hundred and eighty-one rangers snowshoed past Fort Ticonderoga. One hundred and eighty-one rangers started coming in on Crown Point, trekking slowly on their bulky snowshoes in a bitter wind. Then, suddenly, they sighted Abenaki and French skating down a river below them.

Rogers signaled: attack! And the rangers halloed and swung down on them like flocks of angry geese. Suddenly new shots thundered. The first troops had been only an advance guard! Hundreds more French and Indians were coming at the rangers. The missing provincial soldier must have spilled the plans!

Whooping wildly, the French and Abenaki started firing into the trapped rangers. It was three to two. The rangers took to the trees. But there weren't enough trees, and it was almost impossible to run with their snowshoes. Smoke plumed up from the musket fire. The French and Abenaki grappled with the trapped rangers. Bayonet to bayonet. Knife to knife. Hand to hand.

"*Sereeeeeeet!*" Rogers whistled, motioning the rangers up the hill toward the lake. From tree to tree they sprang. But the French and Indians sprang after them. Rogers backed up farther. "Scatter!" he shouted to the others.

Then he turned and ran. Suddenly he stopped. He was at the top of a cliff. An impossible cliff! It dropped hundreds of feet to Lake George, and the Indians were still coming.

Quickly, he slipped off his jacket and . . . jumped.
But where?
The Indians weren't at all sure. They sneaked up slowly and looked behind the trees. They looked behind the rocks. Then they looked over the cliff. No man could jump over that cliff—and live!

A Frenchman stumbled over the coat, picked it up and

discovered the very letter General Shirley had given
Rogers. The soldier read it, laughing, then shouting.

"Rogers, it was Rogers!"

That night the French commander chuckled with glee
and toasted. "Rogers is killed completely, clothes, coat
and breeches!"

But Rogers was no more dead than the commander
himself. By then he had sneaked through the woods to
meet the rangers who had escaped. Five hours later he
was pacing in front of the fire in his hut.

For years after, people wondered: did Rogers really
jump off that terrible cliff and escape?

"Certainly," Rogers would say with a grin.

But, to tell the truth, it's never been clear. What was clear was that no one had killed Major Robert Rogers. Not that day.

But they had killed a part of him. One hundred and seventeen rangers had been killed or captured. Worst of all, some had been tortured first by the Abenaki. So instead of being humbled, as Colonel Haviland perhaps hoped, Rogers was spitting mad. Mad at the Frenchmen, but even more mad at the Abenaki.

The rangers would attack again all right. In his mind he even decided where! But first he had to convince someone to let him lead an attack again.

A new general, General Howe, mumbled, "We need to cut the enemy line to Lake Champlain."

"The rangers can do it, Sir," Rogers said.

"Perhaps an attack on Crown Point," mused General Abercromby.

"The rangers are right for that attack, sir!"

"Now, here, near Ticonderoga, if we waged a battle here...," pointed out General Amherst.

"Sir, just the move for the rangers!"

Rogers even wrote letters, sometimes hinting where he felt the attack should be. But to all his pleadings the generals said no. No. No. No. Regular soldiers would do it.

In July 1758, when the regulars finally did attack Fort Carillon—20,000 of them in 1,000 boats—General

Abercromby did let Rogers and his rangers scout ahead for them.

And though the British lost that battle, the new general, Jeffery Amherst, asked the rangers to lead all the British armies a year later against Fort Carillon, then Crown Point. They won both times.

But make an attack alone?

Not on your life! Not until September 1759, when General Amherst got mad, as only a general can, were the rangers ordered out on their own. That was the time the Abenaki had captured two of his officers who were carrying a white flag of truce. (They were really spies, disguised as peace carriers, but Amherst neglected to admit that.) The general got furious and ordered Rogers to attack.

Where? Suagothel.

6

Robert Rogers could be stubborn, impossibly stubborn, about a whole lot of things. But never was he more stubborn than in keeping the secret of "Suagothel." He didn't tell—wouldn't tell—anyone where it was. And he didn't plan to. Not until the right time.

He went to bed that night alone, knowing Suagothel was St. Francis, the main village of the Abenaki.

"Suagothel!" He rolled the word over his tongue and grinned.

It was a peculiar thing about Rogers and the Abenaki. How he hated them! Yet he admired them. He fought them. Yet he copied them. Almost every notion he ever got in his head had something to do with the Abenaki. And, surely, he was the white man they hunted most; they even called him Wabo-Madahondo, "the white devil." Sometimes it almost seemed like a game between Rogers and the Abenaki. A deadly game, to be sure.

Now here was Rogers' chance to win.

He didn't know a lot of things. St. Francis, Suagothel, was one hundred and fifty miles away, but one hundred fifty miles of what? Were there mountains to cross?

Ravines? Rivers? He wasn't sure. It had never been charted. But he was sure what he would do when he got there, and he was sure that nothing would stop him and his rangers this time.

It was September 13, 1759, when 182 men—rangers, some provincials, some regulars—set off in their whale-boats with only their backpacks, their compasses and their muskets. Past enemy boats.

Swip, pull. Swip, pull.

Ten days.

They hid the boats in the thicket, then hiked through woods so thick it seemed like night.

Two days.

Through spruce bogs so damp and wet, Rogers had to show them how to make a hammock of branches and sleep in the trees.

Nine days.

Through weather so cold, their pants stiffened with frost and their shirts froze on their backs.

On and on and on Rogers kept them going. Ninety miles. A hundred miles. Marching, slogging, pulling themselves through the thicket, staggering to keep up with the growing feeling *they were being followed.*

Until they reached the brown and churning St. Francis River. Finally, forming a human chain, they passed their guns across, then themselves. It was October 4. They were 15 miles from the village of St. Francis.

In early evening the next day Rogers left the rangers

to spy on the village. Crouched in a tree, he saw it. Small huts, a chapel, scalps hanging from poles—the sight enraged him! He crept back and just before dawn threw the signal to attack.

Like shadows, the rangers slipped silently into the sleeping village. Then in a sudden wave the rangers surged. They battered down doors. They shot at braves who flew toward their canoes. They fought hand to hand with those who didn't. They tore into the church, battering it as they went. Then they rounded up the women and children and some white captives and set fire to the village.

The fire leaped like an angry dragon, lurching from hut to hut. It cracked. It sizzled, the light flickering on the frightened faces.

So many thoughts crowded Rogers' head as he watched the fire. Of his cabin long ago in ashes. Of his rangers lying dead in the snow. Thoughts. Yes, he was stubborn, impossibly stubborn, but his plan had worked. The Abenaki wouldn't be fighting and raiding the English for a long while. Finally.

But Rogers didn't pause long.

A white captive sneaked up to tell him that all the warriors had not been in camp. A whole war party—maybe 200 strong—was out tracking Rogers' trail! There *had* been someone following them.

The rangers whispered to one another. What would they do? They couldn't go back the way they had come then. The Abenaki were on that trail! They were trapped. Trapped!

But Rogers buckled on his belt and knapsack and called a meeting with his officers. Knowing the Abenaki as he did, he had even guessed they might track the rangers! He shared his ideas with the officers, then turned back to the waiting faces and snapped his fingers.

"You. You. You." He pointed to five Abenaki children to follow him. If he had Abenaki children, the warriors wouldn't attack so quickly.

Next he took out his powder horn with the compass in the end. Here was the plan. They wouldn't go back the way they had come. They'd go east. Through the mountains.

He told them he had even made plans for soldiers to bring food up beyond the mountains, to a place where the Connecticut and Wells rivers met. Only 120 miles, he figured. (One hundred and twenty miles!) They'd make it all right, he told them.

"Fill up your sacks with corn!" he shouted. (Some of the rangers filled them up with silver crosses and coins and trinkets instead.) Then, setting his jaw firm, Rogers heisted his gun on his shoulder and stalked out of the smoldering village at a good clip.

Why should anything stop them? He obviously had everything planned. Those warriors wouldn't attack so quickly—not with the children among the rangers. The rangers had become used to the pace, so they'd have no trouble marching. The weather was better, sunny. Now they had food in their pouches, and they'd catch game along the way, so they wouldn't go hungry. And at the Wells River they'd find fresh supplies—salt pork, peas, biscuits. . . .

But as they marched and marched and marched through rocky riverbeds and brambly woods, a whole lot of things started happening that Robert Rogers never planned on.

The weather turned bitter, growing colder by the hour, sinking into a winterlike fog. At night the rangers and captives and Indian children huddled together without a fire. (The Indians would see the smoke.)

Days they faced a sleeting rain.

No ranger tricks fooled the Abenaki, not even their having the Indian children. By the second night, when the troop huddled together, the Abenaki were all around them, waiting. *Hoot. Hoot . . . hooot. Whippoor-will. Whippoor-will.* Every huddled ranger, every captive, every child knew these were not birds.

Worst of all, the tiny troop was hungry. As thick as the woods were, the rangers saw not a single deer. Only a few rabbits and squirrels. Almost nothing to trap or shoot. And while Rogers' sack was filled with corn, too many rangers had not packed corn. They had indeed packed silver trinkets, and they couldn't eat silver trinkets.

Their stomachs ached. Six days passed, seven. They started seeing deer that weren't there, shooting blindly, stumbling, crying. One ranger frantically pulled off his belt . . . and ate it. Another ate his leather sack. They were that hungry!

Finally, the major and the rangers decided to split into small parties, thinking they'd find deer or rabbit or squirrel more easily that way. Instead, they found the Abenaki were only waiting for them to separate. There were screams in the night. Five rangers and two Indian hostages were captured, one party disappeared, another party finally stumbled back to Rogers.

Still they marched, shivering from the quarrelsome winds, and shirts damp from the mists and fogs and light snow. The children stumbled after the rangers, trying to keep up, sharing the rangers' corn, huddling with them through the impossibly long cold nights.

"The Wells River is only eighty miles away," Rogers told them and then, "It's only forty miles now," and again, "Keep going; it's only thirty miles away."

There were no enemies among them. There couldn't be. They were counting on each other to stay alive.

"You'll make it," Rogers whispered to the children, to the captive dragging behind, to the hungry ranger. "You'll make it." He said those same words over and over.

But not everyone did make it. By the time they had marched 110 miles, 24 rangers and a captive had dropped along the way, too hungry or sick to go on. It looked as if they would not make it to the Wells River.

———◆◆———

But the major became the more stubborn. That last night, as he divided the last handful of corn among the survivors, he looked each of them in the eyes and said it a last time: "We will make it."

And they went to sleep, a shivering knot of people, thinking, yes, they would make it. The major had said so. And in the morning, before noon, they did make it. They ran down the last hill toward the place where the Wells and Connecticut rivers met. They ran and stumbled and laughed because ahead they could see a smoldering fire. The soldiers had come! With the food! Probably whole packages of it—salt pork to boil into hot, thick soup; biscuits, maybe; maybe rice—that would be filling.

But when they stopped at the dying fire, there was nothing there. And no one. Rogers' eyes grew round. Angrily, he pulled the bushes aside and shot his gun into the air.

"Where are you?" he shouted. But only the rivers tumbling over the rocks answered him. "Where are you!" he shouted again.

But there was no answer.

7

If there had been anyone at the Wells River, he had gone.

The Indian boy hid his face. The women dropped their heads between their knees. Even some of the rangers slumped to the ground. Not Rogers. He was fuming! Someone had erred. He'd have their neck! But for now, he wasn't going to come this far and be stopped. He said he and his rangers would make it. And, by Gad, they would!

He dropped to his knees. "Here," he said, scruffling through the bed of leaves. "A lily bulb. Boil it and eat. It's bitter but it will fill your stomach. And here. Here's another."

Several rangers started digging, too. The rest of the weary troupe looked up under gray brows and eagerly clutched the banquet that Rogers and his rangers were discovering for them. Then Rogers stared at them hard, almost angrily.

"Now, you dig, too, and keep digging. I'll be back."

The whole adventure was stretching out like taffy before a fire.

Major Rogers picked two rangers and the Abenaki boy, Sabbatis, and they started off for the Connecticut River. The colonial frontier fort, Fort Number Four, was a hundred miles downstream.

"We'll just have to get there," he told them.

First, without axes or saws, they burned five small trees near the base and toppled them. Then they cut vines for twine and put together a raft.

Pushing off into the rapids, they were carried swiftly down the river. Perhaps for once something would happen quickly, easily. Rogers stretched out on the raft, his hands beneath his head. The others lay on their stomachs, their backs to the sun. They basked like turtles on a muddy log carried downstream, steering only now and then with a branch.

But not for long. Suddenly, their raft turned into a spin. Falls-like rapids. Another whirlpool grabbed them and flung them into a frothy pit. Finally, the river threw the raft up into the air, and the major and the rangers, grasping their muskets, toppled into the river. Sabbatis plunged in after them.

Desperately gasping for air, they scrambled onto the bank.

On the second day Rogers shook his partners awake. "Get up." His voice was raspy. "Get up!" Weak as children, after two days without any food, they crawled into the woods to make a new raft. Once more they burned small trees to proper lengths, and banding them together,

again pushed off into the river below the falls.

The river flowed gently, easily here. Perhaps now. . . .

But again, before an hour was out, they heard the thunder of rapids.

"Paddle!" Rogers bellowed. He wasn't going to let the river steal the raft again!

And the four of them paddled the raft ashore, escaping the falls by inches.

They sat at the shore, the water lapping around them. The raft was safe, but too heavy to carry. And they had no strength left to build another. How could they get it past the falls?

On the third morning Rogers shook them awake to tell them how. He placed the three of them above the falls, holding the raft by a vine. Then he waded into the river below the falls. Finally, with the raging waters pulling and tugging at his feet and legs, he shouted, "Let it go!"

Clutching the vine, the rangers and Sabbatis let the raft go. It dipped and reared into the rapids like a stallion. Crazily. Madly. Through the 300 yards, when finally it veered near Rogers.

He stretched out his arms. The raft seemed to dodge, but no raft would outwit him. He leaped into the rapids. Finally he caught and held the careening raft, and swam it through the quieter waters to shore.

On the fourth day the sky was gray and heavy when the four of them floated downstream, wet, the icy air burrowing into their cold damp shirts. The Indian boy lay close to the major. It would snow.

The men who sighted the raft were woodchoppers.

"Are you alive?" they yelled out.

The major nodded. "Just."

In twenty minutes the major, the two rangers and Sabbatis came into Fort Number Four, a low wooden fort on the edge of the river.

"Rest!" the colonels and captains ordered Rogers, as he drank a steaming cup of rum. But they didn't know just how impossible Rogers could be. Particularly when it came to his rangers.

Within a half hour of arriving at the fort, he had rounded up supplies—salt pork, peas, johnny cake—and dry clothes to be sent up to the rangers and captives at Wells River. (They came into the fort four days later.) The next day he himself went back up the river to look for his lost rangers, his good rangers, his remarkable rangers.

Again, Robert Rogers stood ten feet tall!

8

Forty-nine rangers never came back. Perhaps they were killed; perhaps they died of starvation. In the next year Abenaki Indians who were left set up in a neighboring village and went right on fighting alongside the French. But only for a year. The British (the rangers included) finally attacked Montreal and won it, and that pretty much ended the war. After a hundred years of on-and-off war between the French and British, all of Canada fell to the British Crown. That was in 1760.

Suddenly there was no war.

Most people in the British colonies were happy about that. But it wasn't so simple for Robert Rogers. Suddenly there was nothing to ask for. Nothing to train troops for. Nothing to hate. Nothing to love. Nothing to fight.

At first, it looked like the only thing there was for him at the ripe old age of 29 was plenty of trouble.

He had been so busy fighting the French and Abenaki and raising companies and training men and writing letters and begging generals, that he hadn't paid nearly enough attention to money. When the colonies didn't pay him and his men back in 1755, why, he borrowed without

blinking. Sometimes the British forgot to pay him and his men, too. Other times they paid late. So he borrowed some more.

All in all he borrowed 6,000 pounds; that would be about 300,000 dollars. Back in 1760 that was a particularly large amount of money, and suddenly, with the war over, everyone wanted the money back. At once.

Then to confuse matters, Robert Rogers, the soldier, the scrapper, the bullheaded stubborn Rogers, fell in love. With Elizabeth Browne, a fair and proper and fine lady of Portsmouth. And he married her. "Dearest Betsey," he called her.

But in the end, his "dearest Betsey" cost him money, too. His own father-in-law sued him for "2,500 pounds for lodging and support of his daughter." You may be sure that Robert Rogers wished he could come up with a notion or two right then.

But Robert Rogers was not finished yet, as impossible as his troubles seemed. Before he met and married Betsey, he was called in to travel to the wilderness posts to tell them all the English had won. This was in 1760. He paddled through Lake Erie, took over Detroit, sent rangers to forts in Indiana. In 1763, after his marriage, he returned and helped defend Fort Detroit against the Ottawa Indians and their friends.

Then, with some fresh ideas in his head, he sailed to England, where he wrote and sold a play. *Ponteach*, he called it. He wrote and sold his journals of his ranger days.

Journal, he called that. And he wrote and sold his ideas on the Indians and the North American countryside. *A Concise Account* he called it, not that it was any too concise.

While he was there, a good many people made a fuss over "the famous major." That's what they called him—"the famous major." And he got to feeling he could do the impossible all over again. When he met the king for tea (that was George III), he told the king that he should have a superintendent at Fort Michilimackinac. Someone who knew Indians. Someone who could be a sort of British head of all the Indians to the West.

The king believed him, and said to try it out. If it worked, he'd pay him.

So Rogers went to Michilimackinac. (He took his dearest Betsey with him.) And, oh, he rode high! He was the famous Major Rogers all over again. He set the rugged palisade fort up as if he were a kind of ranger king. There were dances in a ballroom, billiards in a billiard room, splendid dinners with tablecloths and candles.

He talked daily with the Indians—all kinds: Hurons, Sioux, Chippewas. Ten years of trading and fighting the Abenaki had made him understand a lot about them. That they needed blankets, coats, wampum. That they wanted guarantees of peace from the king across the sea.

One July he had a great huge powwow of chiefs from as far away as Iowa. He sat with the feather-bonneted leaders and smoked the pipe of peace. They called him "our father, next to the king" and he called them "my brothers."

And he dealt with French traders and soldiers and settlers as well.

But Rogers being Rogers, started getting ideas again. About how someday he and some Rangers would go West, and with help from their Indian friends, they'd discover riches there. Stories said there were mountains of copper, land so fertile corn could grow ten feet high, streams were gold ran—and a trail all the way to the Pacific Ocean.

It was when he shared some of these dreams with Indians and traders that his world started to fold in on him.

Over the years, along with his debts, he had added up a list of enemies that wouldn't fit on a page—little enemies like Benjamin Roberts, the commissary who wanted Rogers' position; bigger enemies, like his secretary, Nathaniel Potter, whom Rogers may have ignored too much. Then there were big enemies like Sir William Johnson (the same general who had been his friend) and General Thomas Gage. Gage never had done too well with that regular light infantry troop that was supposed to replace the rangers, and for some reason he never did forgive Rogers for it.

When word leaked out that Rogers had these dreams, those enemies, some big and some small, put their heads together and decided Rogers needed to be toppled from his wooden throne. They said he planned treason against

the king, that he plotted to join his old enemies, the French and Indians, and then head West.

This time not even his quick tongue could save Robert Rogers, and on December 6, 1767, he was arrested in the courtyard at the fort and thrown into chains in a cold and drafty cell. Only Betsey could talk to him. All his papers—evidence—were taken and he was kept in irons so heavy that he nearly fainted when he tried to walk with them.

Nearly a year later he was sent to Montreal to stand trial. He insisted on defending himself.

Bony and thin, the old spirit flushed briefly in his face as he stood up that day after hearing his accusers. He looked around the court, which had grown strangely still. Then he began to speak, his voice quivering angrily.

"I was thrown into jail without any examination!

"I was loaded with irons!

"I was arrested for being a traitor to the king, yet no one has even mentioned that in this trial today!"

His voice grew steadier, sterner as he went on.

"I was not allowed to bring any evidence on the ship here!

"I have not been allowed to ask any questions of my accusers in this trial!"

Now the voice was the voice of Major Rogers, the ranger. Even the face grew strong. The eyes. Angry. Stubborn. Robert Rogers then began to answer his accusers. He had never betrayed his king. He had never made plans to betray his king. And until anyone found proof that he had, he had to be found not guilty! *Not guilty!*

Then, finally, the hush. When the judges reentered the room, the chief justice's tone was tired but firm when he read,

"We find Major Rogers . . . not guilty!"

In a way, Rogers had won. In a way, he still was the loser. He was no longer superintendent. He was sick from months in jail. He owed more people than ever since the British Crown had never paid him. And when he went back to England for help, the army of people he owed money finally caught up with him.

In 1772, Roberts Rogers, the famous major, the clever woodsman, the soldier, the impossible Robert Rogers, landed in the rat-infested Fleet Street Jail in London.

He did get out—three years later. He went back to America, but times had changed. It was 1775. And since he was still considered a British major, he was considered an enemy. When he tried to join General Washington's army, he was turned down flatly. A spy, they said.

So again, out of money and friends (his wife even divorced him in 1778), he joined the British army and fought with it for three years in the Revolution. But not with his whole heart, and he finally returned to England.

After that he drifted into dingy pubs, taverns, drinking too much ale and bragging boisterously of those days—

those other days when he had this notion in his head that a band of woodsmen could fight in the wilderness like Indians. Rangers, he called them.

Not ten feet tall at all, but a tired and worn and disappointed old man, Robert Rogers died on May 8, 1795, a world away from the wilderness that had made him.

AUTHOR'S NOTE

Robert Rogers not only was an impossible man, he was mysterious as well. There are parts of his life about which we can only guess. We know, for example, that Rogers was a defendant in the counterfeiting trial, but his exact role is still somewhat obscure. We know Robert Rogers knew the New England wilderness expertly, but it was only a studied guess by historian Francis Parkman that led to the conclusion that Rogers became familiar with the wilderness while smuggling goods between the French and English colonies.

Some of the mysteries are created by time. How much money did Rogers owe, for example? What does 5,000 pounds mean in terms of our money? Since the value of our money fluctuates from year to year, month to month, we can only make an approximate calculation. I used the value of an 18th-century pound against a 1960 dollar.

There is no mystery, however, about the influence Robert Rogers had on the American Revolution. While he himself fought on the British side because of George Washington's refusal to have him, he influenced the Patriots nonetheless. His fighting methods were taken up by the Patriot army, which frequently adapted the light infantry-ranger form of warfare. John Stark, Rogers' best friend and lieutenant, led and won the famous battle of Bennington in 1777.

Perhaps it is the mystery and impossibility of the man that keeps his name alive even today, as an echo in the wilderness of the Champlain Valley, and with people who love adventure everywhere.